Let's learn patterns so we will know what comes next!

Patterns

Patterns are things-numbers, shapes, images-that repeat in a logical way.

Patterns help us to learn to make predictions, to understand what comes next, to make logical connections, and to use reasoning skills.

What Comes Next? Logic Patterns

Math Books for Grade 1
Children's Math Books

BABY PROFESSOR

EDUCATION KIDS

Speedy Publishing LLC
40 E. Main St. #1156
Newark, DE 19711
www.speedypublishing.com
Copyright 2017

Completing Pattern

Circle the picture that comes next in each picture.

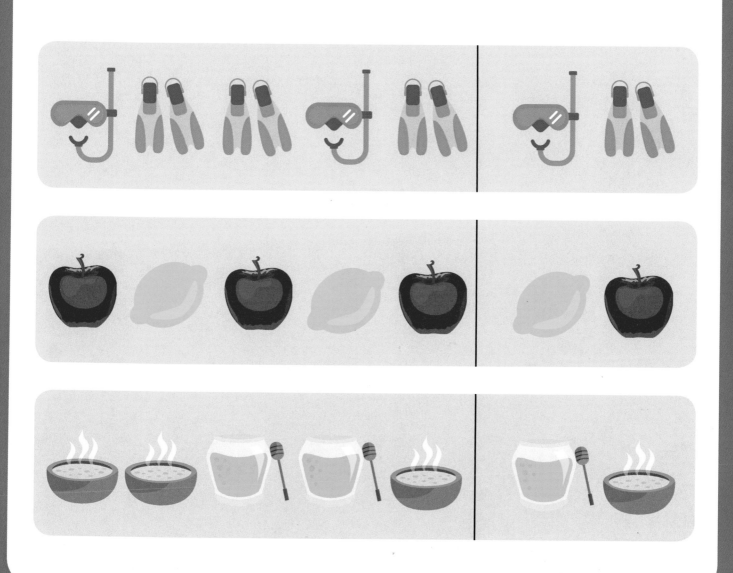

Completing Pattern

Circle the picture that comes next in each picture.

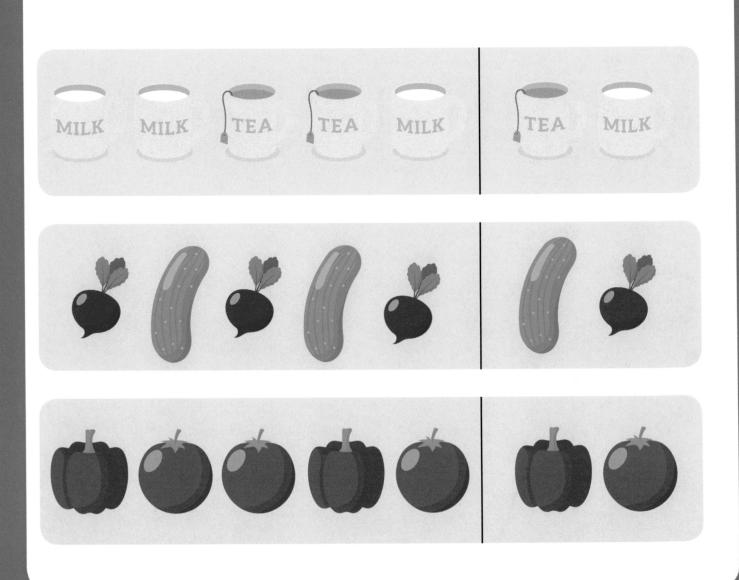

Completing Pattern

Circle the picture that comes next in each picture.

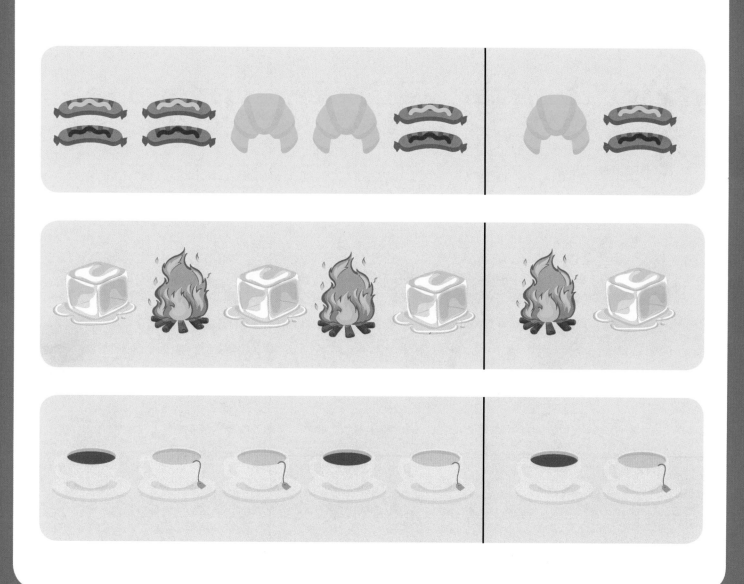

Completing Pattern

Circle the picture that comes next in each picture.

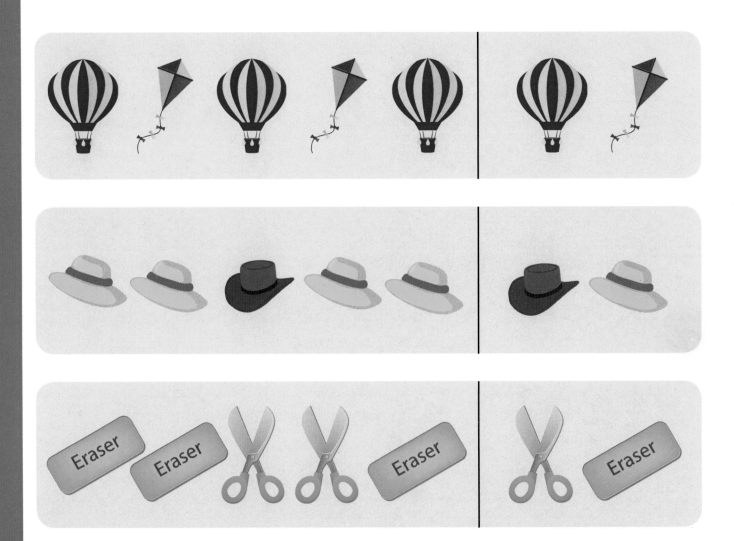

Completing Pattern

Circle the picture that comes next in each picture.

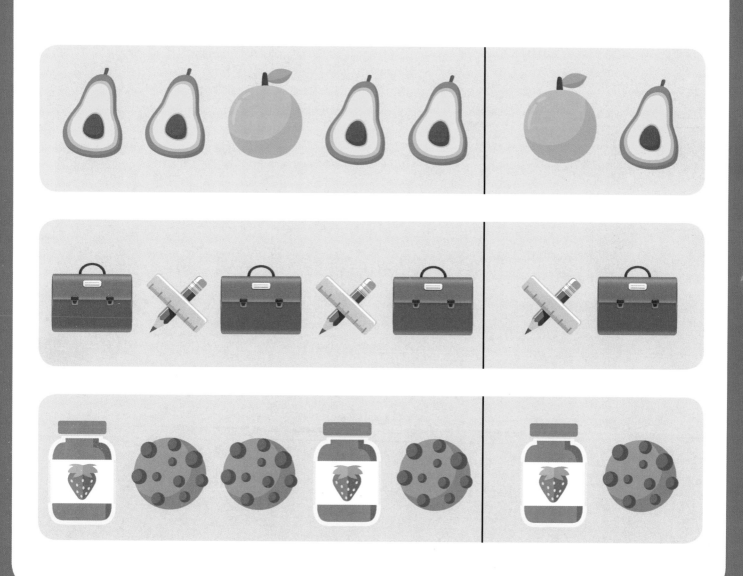

Completing Pattern

Circle the picture that comes next in each picture.

Completing Pattern

Circle the picture that comes next in each picture.

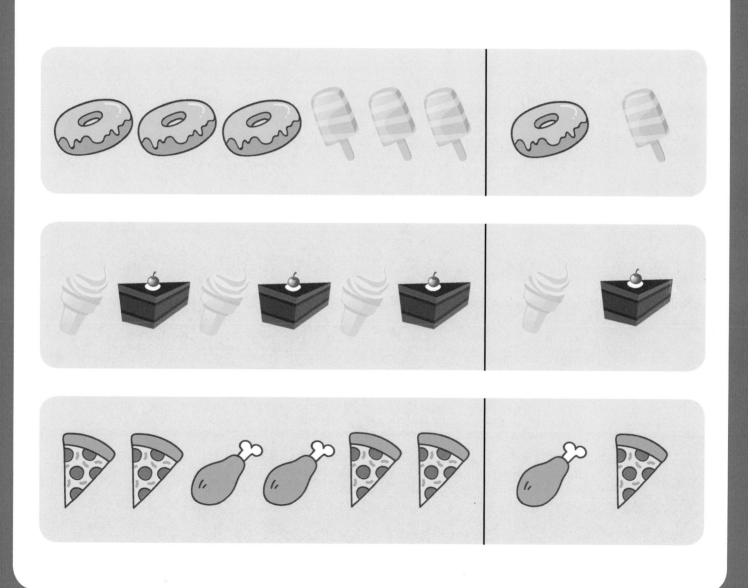

Completing Pattern

Circle the picture that comes next in each picture.

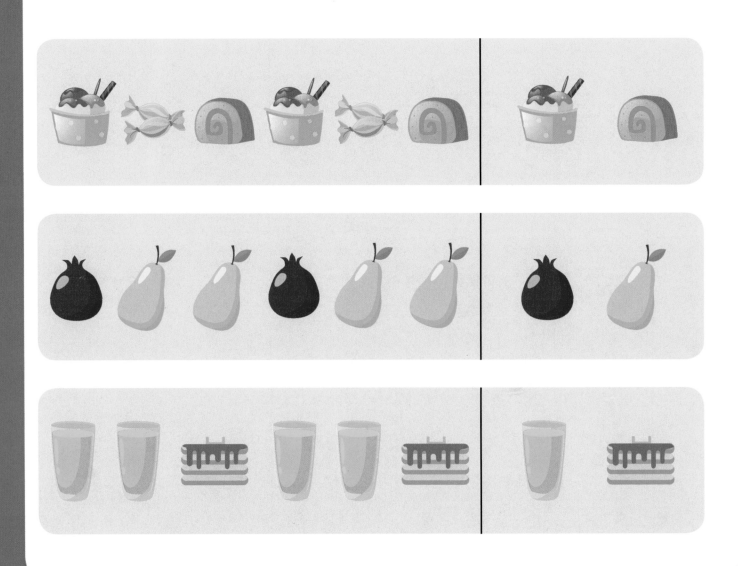

Completing Pattern

Circle the picture that comes next in each picture.

Identifying Number Series

Identify the number pattern and fill in the missing numbers.

1. | 2 | 4 | 6 | 8 | 10 | |

2. | 17 | 19 | 21 | 23 | 25 | |

3. | 48 | 44 | 40 | 36 | 32 | |

4. | 10 | 15 | 20 | 25 | 30 | |

Identifying Number Series

Identify the number pattern and fill in the missing numbers.

5. | 27 | 25 | 23 | 21 | 19 | |

6. | 6 | 12 | 18 | 24 | 30 | |

7. | 1 | 3 | 5 | 7 | 9 | |

8. | 40 | 38 | 36 | 34 | 32 | |

Identifying Number Series

Identify the number pattern and fill in the missing numbers.

9. | 12 | 15 | 18 | 21 | 24 | |

10. | 32 | 30 | 28 | 24 | 22 | |

11. | 3 | 5 | 7 | 9 | 11 | |

12. | 22 | 20 | 18 | 16 | 14 | |

Identifying Number Series

Identify the number pattern and fill in the missing numbers.

13. | 5 | 10 | 15 | 20 | 25 | |

14. | 12 | 14 | 16 | 18 | 20 | |

15. | 77 | 70 | 63 | 56 | 49 | |

16. | 3 | 6 | 9 | 12 | 15 | |

Identifying Number Series

Identify the number pattern and fill in the missing numbers.

17. | 78 | 72 | 66 | 60 | 54 | |

18. | 27 | 29 | 31 | 33 | 35 | |

19. | 20 | 24 | 28 | 32 | 36 | |

20. | 39 | 36 | 33 | 30 | 27 | |

Identifying Number Series

Identify the number pattern and fill in the missing numbers.

21. | 55 | 50 | 45 | 40 | 35 | |

22. | 4 | 6 | 8 | 10 | 12 | |

23. | 26 | 24 | 22 | 20 | 18 | |

24. | 6 | 12 | 18 | 24 | 30 | |

Identifying Number Series

Identify the number pattern and fill in the missing numbers.

25. | 11 | 13 | 15 | 17 | 19 | |

26. | 64 | 60 | 56 | 52 | 48 | |

27. | 74 | 72 | 70 | 68 | 66 | |

28. | 10 | 15 | 20 | 25 | 30 | |

Identifying Number Series

Identify the number pattern and fill in the missing numbers.

29.

48	45	42	39	36	

30.

16	20	24	28	32	

31.

-11	-9	-7	-5	-3	

32.

4	8	12	16	20	

Identifying Number Series

Identify the number pattern and fill in the missing numbers.

33. | 60 | 50 | 40 | 30 | 20 | |

34. | -24 | -22 | -20 | -18 | -16 | |

35. | 12 | 15 | 18 | 21 | 24 | |

36. | 25 | 20 | 15 | 10 | 5 | |

Identifying Number Series

Identify the number pattern and fill in the missing numbers.

37. | 62 | 64 | 66 | 68 | 70 | |

38. | -21 | -18 | -15 | -12 | -9 | |

39. | 6 | 12 | 18 | 24 | 30 | |

40. | 15 | 10 | 5 | 0 | -5 | |

Identifying Number Series

Identify the number pattern and fill in the missing numbers.

41. | 22 | 20 | 18 | 16 | 14 | |

42. | -5 | -3 | -1 | 1 | 3 | |

43. | 40 | 30 | 20 | 10 | 0 | |

44. | 14 | 16 | 18 | 20 | 22 | |

Identifying Number Series

Identify the number pattern and fill in the missing numbers.

45. | 96 | 88 | 80 | 72 | 64 | |

46. | -35 | -30 | -25 | -20 | -15 | |

47. | 13 | 11 | 9 | 7 | 5 | |

48. | 21 | 18 | 15 | 12 | 9 | |

Identifying Number Series

Identify the number pattern and fill in the missing numbers.

49. | 7 | 14 | 21 | 28 | 35 | |

50. | -2 | -4 | -6 | -8 | -10 | |

51. | 3 | 6 | 9 | 12 | 15 | |

52. | 23 | 21 | 19 | 17 | 15 | |

Identifying Number Series

Identify the number pattern and fill in the missing numbers.

53. | -10 | -8 | -6 | -4 | -2 | |
    |-----|----|----|----|----|--|

54. | 5 | 10 | 15 | 20 | 25 | |
    |---|----|----|----|----|--|

55. | 18 | 15 | 12 | 9 | 6 | |
    |----|----|----|---|---|--|

56. | 32 | 36 | 40 | 44 | 48 | |
    |----|----|----|----|----|--|

Identifying Number Series

Identify the number pattern and fill in the missing numbers.

57. | -10 | -12 | -14 | -16 | -18 | |

58. | 84 | 77 | 70 | 63 | 56 | |

59. | -9 | -6 | -3 | 0 | 3 | |

60. | 20 | 10 | 0 | -10 | -20 | |

Identifying Number Series

Identify the number pattern and fill in the missing numbers.

61. | 10 | 12 | 14 | 16 | 18 | |

62. | 25 | 27 | 29 | 31 | 33 | |

63. | 32 | 28 | 24 | 20 | 16 | |

Identifying Number Series

Identify the number pattern and fill in the missing numbers.

Count by 2 from 7 to 23

			13		17			23

Count by 1 from 5 to 13

		7	8			11		

Identifying Number Series

Identify the number pattern and fill in the missing numbers.

Count by 2 from 1 to 17

				9	11			17

Count by 1 from 3 to 11

	4		6	7				

Identifying Number Series

Identify the number pattern and fill in the missing numbers.

Count by 4 from 10 to 42

				26	30			42

Count by 3 from 7 to 31

				19			28	31

Identifying Number Series

Identify the number pattern and fill in the missing numbers.

Count by 1 from 6 to 14

		8	9				13	

Count by 5 from 6 to 46

6					31			46

Identifying Number Series

Identify the number pattern and fill in the missing numbers.

Count by 1 from 2 to 10

	3	4					10

Count by 2 from 10 to 26

10					22	26

Identifying Number Series

Identify the number pattern and fill in the missing numbers.

Count by 2 from 6 to 22

| 6 | 8 | | | 14 | | | |

Count by 3 from 4 to 28

| 4 | 7 | | | | | 22 | |

Identifying Number Series

Identify the number pattern and fill in the missing numbers.

Count by 4 from 7 to 39

7		15					39

Count by 1 from 5 to 13

				9	10		12	

Identifying Number Series

Identify the number pattern and fill in the missing numbers.

Count by 3 from 1 to 25

					16	19		25

Count by 2 from 1 to 17

		5					15	17

Identifying Number Series

Identify the number pattern and fill in the missing numbers.

Count by 1 from 48 to 41

	47			43		

Count by 3 from 43 to 22

			34			25	

Identifying Number Series

Identify the number pattern and fill in the missing numbers.

Count by 2 from 47 to 33

			41			35	

Count by 1 from 33 to 26

33						27	

Identifying Number Series

Identify the number pattern and fill in the missing numbers.

Count by 1 from 42 to 35

		40				35

Count by 3 from 45 to 24

			36			24

Identifying Number Series

Identify the number pattern and fill in the missing numbers.

Count by 1 from 35 to 28

	34		32				

Count by 2 from 45 to 31

	43			37			

Answer keys

Completing Pattern

Circle the picture that comes next in each picture.

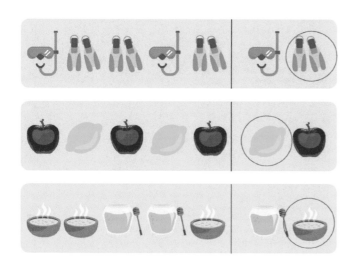

Completing Pattern

Circle the picture that comes next in each picture.

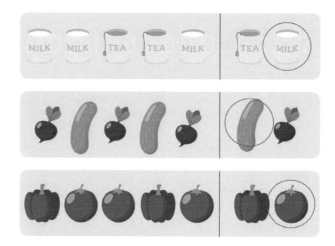

Completing Pattern
Circle the picture that comes next in each picture.

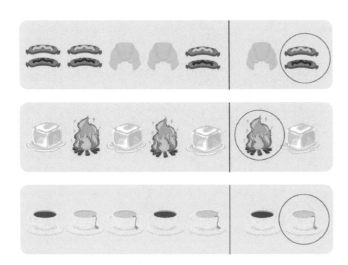

Completing Pattern
Circle the picture that comes next in each picture.

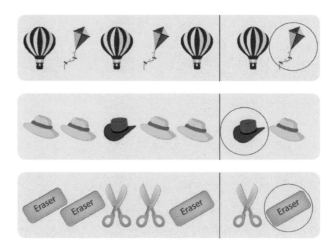

Completing Pattern

Circle the picture that comes next in each picture.

Completing Pattern

Circle the picture that comes next in each picture.

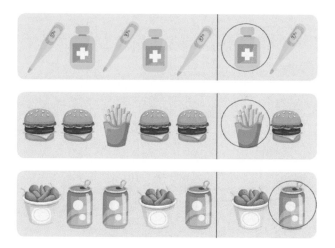

Completing Pattern

Circle the picture that comes next in each picture.

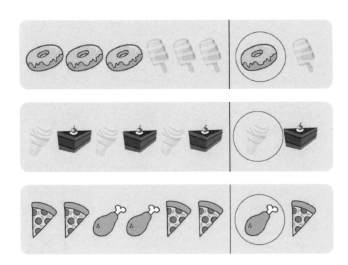

Completing Pattern

Circle the picture that comes next in each picture.

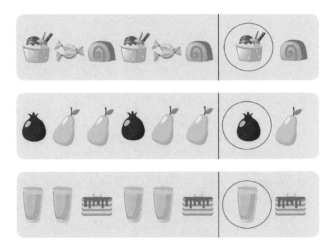

Circle the picture that comes next in each picture.

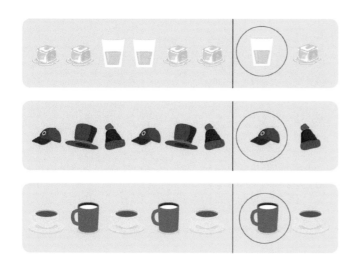

Identifying Number Series

Identify the number pattern and fill in the missing numbers.

1. | 2 | 4 | 6 | 8 | 10 | 2 |

2. | 17 | 19 | 21 | 23 | 25 | 27 |

3. | 48 | 44 | 40 | 36 | 32 | 28 |

4. | 10 | 15 | 20 | 25 | 30 | 35 |

Identifying Number Series

Identify the number pattern and fill in the missing numbers.

5. | 27 | 25 | 23 | 21 | 19 | 17 |

6. | 6 | 12 | 18 | 24 | 30 | 36 |

7. | 1 | 3 | 5 | 7 | 9 | 11 |

8. | 40 | 38 | 36 | 34 | 32 | 30 |

Identifying Number Series

Identify the number pattern and fill in the missing numbers.

9. | 12 | 15 | 18 | 21 | 24 | 27 |

10. | 32 | 30 | 28 | 24 | 22 | 20 |

11. | 3 | 5 | 7 | 9 | 11 | 13 |

12. | 22 | 20 | 18 | 16 | 14 | 12 |

Identifying Number Series

Identify the number pattern and fill in the missing numbers.

13. | 5 | 10 | 15 | 20 | 25 | 30 |

14. | 12 | 14 | 16 | 18 | 20 | 22 |

15. | 77 | 70 | 63 | 56 | 49 | 42 |

16. | 3 | 6 | 9 | 12 | 15 | 18 |

Identifying Number Series

Identify the number pattern and fill in the missing numbers.

17. | 78 | 72 | 66 | 60 | 54 | 48 |

18. | 27 | 29 | 31 | 33 | 35 | 37 |

19. | 20 | 24 | 28 | 32 | 36 | 40 |

20. | 39 | 36 | 33 | 30 | 27 | 24 |

Identifying Number Series

Identify the number pattern and fill in the missing numbers.

21. | 55 | 50 | 45 | 40 | 35 | 30 |

22. | 4 | 6 | 8 | 10 | 12 | 14 |

23. | 26 | 24 | 22 | 20 | 18 | 16 |

24. | 6 | 12 | 18 | 24 | 30 | 36 |

Identifying Number Series

Identify the number pattern and fill in the missing numbers.

25. | 11 | 13 | 15 | 17 | 19 | 21 |

26. | 64 | 60 | 56 | 52 | 48 | 44 |

27. | 74 | 72 | 70 | 68 | 66 | 64 |

28. | 10 | 15 | 20 | 25 | 30 | 35 |

Identifying Number Series

Identify the number pattern and fill in the missing numbers.

29. | 48 | 45 | 42 | 39 | 36 | 33 |

30. | 16 | 20 | 24 | 28 | 32 | 36 |

31. | -11 | -9 | -7 | -5 | -3 | -1 |

32. | 4 | 8 | 12 | 16 | 20 | 24 |

Identifying Number Series

Identify the number pattern and fill in the missing numbers.

33. | 60 | 50 | 40 | 30 | 20 | 10 |

34. | -24 | -22 | -20 | -18 | -16 | -14 |

35. | 12 | 15 | 18 | 21 | 24 | 27 |

36. | 25 | 20 | 15 | 10 | 5 | 0 |

Identifying Number Series

Identify the number pattern and fill in the missing numbers.

37. | 62 | 64 | 66 | 68 | 70 | 72 |

38. | -21 | -18 | -15 | -12 | -9 | -6 |

39. | 6 | 12 | 18 | 24 | 30 | 36 |

40. | 15 | 10 | 5 | 0 | -5 | -10 |

Identifying Number Series

Identify the number pattern and fill in the missing numbers.

41. | 22 | 20 | 18 | 16 | 14 | 12 |

42. | -5 | -3 | -1 | 1 | 3 | 5 |

43. | 40 | 30 | 20 | 10 | 0 | -10 |

44. | 14 | 16 | 18 | 20 | 22 | 24 |

Identifying Number Series

Identify the number pattern and fill in the missing numbers.

45. | 96 | 88 | 80 | 72 | 64 | 56 |

46. | -35 | -30 | -25 | -20 | -15 | -10 |

47. | 13 | 11 | 9 | 7 | 5 | 3 |

48. | 21 | 18 | 15 | 12 | 9 | 6 |

Identifying Number Series

Identify the number pattern and fill in the missing numbers.

49. | 7 | 14 | 21 | 28 | 35 | 42 |

50. | -2 | -4 | -6 | -8 | -10 | -12 |

51. | 3 | 6 | 9 | 12 | 15 | 18 |

52. | 23 | 21 | 19 | 17 | 15 | 13 |

Identifying Number Series

Identify the number pattern and fill in the missing numbers.

53. | -10 | -8 | -6 | -4 | -2 | 0 |

54. | 5 | 10 | 15 | 20 | 25 | 30 |

55. | 18 | 15 | 12 | 9 | 6 | 3 |

56. | 32 | 36 | 40 | 44 | 48 | 52 |

Identifying Number Series

Identify the number pattern and fill in the missing numbers.

57. | -10 | -12 | -14 | -16 | -18 | -20 |

58. | 84 | 77 | 70 | 63 | 56 | 49 |

59. | -9 | -6 | -3 | 0 | 3 | 6 |

60. | 20 | 10 | 0 | -10 | -20 | -30 |

Identifying Number Series

Identify the number pattern and fill in the missing numbers.

61. | 10 | 12 | 14 | 16 | 18 | 20 |

62. | 25 | 27 | 29 | 31 | 33 | 35 |

63. | 32 | 28 | 24 | 20 | 16 | 12 |

64. | 30 | 35 | 40 | 45 | 50 | 55 |

Identifying Number Series

Identify the number pattern and fill in the missing numbers.

Count by 2 from 7 to 23

| 7 | 9 | 11 | 13 | 15 | 17 | 19 | 21 | 23 |

Count by 1 from 5 to 13

| 5 | 6 | 7 | 8 | 9 | 10 | 11 | 12 | 13 |

Identifying Number Series

Identify the number pattern and fill in the missing numbers.

Count by 2 from 1 to 17

| 1 | 3 | 5 | 7 | 9 | 11 | 13 | 15 | 17 |

Count by 1 from 3 to 11

| 3 | 4 | 5 | 6 | 7 | 8 | 9 | 10 | 11 |

Identifying Number Series

Identify the number pattern and fill in the missing numbers.

Count by 4 from 10 to 42

| 10 | 14 | 18 | 22 | 26 | 30 | 34 | 38 | 42 |

Count by 3 from 7 to 31

| 7 | 10 | 13 | 16 | 19 | 22 | 25 | 28 | 31 |

Identifying Number Series

Identify the number pattern and fill in the missing numbers.

Count by 1 from 6 to 14

6	7	8	9	10	11	12	13	14

Count by 5 from 6 to 46

6	11	16	21	26	31	36	41	46

Identifying Number Series

Identify the number pattern and fill in the missing numbers.

Count by 1 from 2 to 10

2	3	4	5	6	7	8	9	10

Count by 2 from 10 to 26

10	12	14	16	18	20	22	24	26

Identifying Number Series

Identify the number pattern and fill in the missing numbers.

Count by 2 from 6 to 22

| 6 | 8 | 10 | 12 | 14 | 16 | 18 | 20 | 22 |

Count by 3 from 4 to 28

| 4 | 7 | 10 | 13 | 16 | 19 | 22 | 25 | 28 |

Identifying Number Series

Identify the number pattern and fill in the missing numbers.

Count by 4 from 7 to 39

| 7 | 11 | 15 | 19 | 23 | 27 | 31 | 35 | 39 |

Count by 1 from 5 to 13

| 5 | 6 | 7 | 8 | 9 | 10 | 11 | 12 | 13 |

Identifying Number Series

Identify the number pattern and fill in the missing numbers.

Count by 3 from 1 to 25

| 1 | 4 | 7 | 10 | 13 | 16 | 19 | 22 | 25 |

Count by 2 from 1 to 17

| 1 | 3 | 5 | 7 | 9 | 11 | 13 | 15 | 17 |

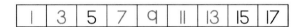

Identifying Number Series

Identify the number pattern and fill in the missing numbers.

Count by 1 from 48 to 41

| 48 | 47 | 46 | 45 | 44 | 43 | 42 | 41 |

Count by 3 from 43 to 22

| 43 | 40 | 37 | 34 | 31 | 28 | 25 | 22 |

Identifying Number Series

Identify the number pattern and fill in the missing numbers.

Count by 2 from 47 to 33

| 47 | 45 | 43 | 41 | 39 | 37 | 35 | 33 |

Count by 1 from 33 to 26

| 33 | 32 | 31 | 30 | 29 | 28 | 27 | 26 |

Identifying Number Series

Identify the number pattern and fill in the missing numbers.

Count by 1 from 42 to 35

| 42 | 41 | 40 | 39 | 38 | 37 | 36 | 35 |

Count by 3 from 45 to 24

| 45 | 42 | 39 | 36 | 33 | 30 | 27 | 24 |

Identifying Number Series

Identify the number pattern and fill in the missing numbers.

Count by 1 from 35 to 28

35	34	33	32	31	30	29	28

Count by 2 from 45 to 31

45	43	41	39	37	35	33	31

Visit

BABY PROFESSOR
EDUCATION KIDS

www.BabyProfessorBooks.com

to download Free Baby Professor eBooks
and view our catalog of new and exciting
Children's Books